HOUDINI

Praise for Roving Eye Press

Avant-garde avatar Bob Brown's literary love letter to Harry Houdini conclusively conjures this preeminent "picker of pockets and padlocks"! Ace academic Craig Saper excitedly elucidates Brown's terrific tribute!

~Barry Mauer, University of Central Florida

Like a madly inspired doctor, Brown prods, pushes, and cuts his words into and out of meaning until — I swear — he might even awake T. S. Eliot's etherized patient. If there was, most often, something slightly clumsy about Brown's insistent linguistic embracements, he seldom shied from his commitment, determining to never abandon his love of words, even if he had to create his "Superb swirling compositions / On my back where even I / Cannot see my masterpieces."

~Douglas Messerli, Green Integer Press

To focus on Brown's relationship to either more famous Modernists like Stein, or to the modern technologies he presaged, deflect from the thorny questions he asked circa 1930, which have been taken up by subsequent avant-gardists. For the challenges he posed to the way we read — challenges we continue to wrestle with today — Bob Brown deserves his own time in the spotlight.

~Steven Wingate, *American Book Review*

Of the many Americans who helped to shape the cultural explosion we call Modernism, few came up to the mark of Bob Brown for sheer 'esprit' and intellectual daring. To read him is to know what intellectual freedom could or should or might truly mean.

~Jerome McGann, University of Virginia

Bob Brown was at the very center of his time, a zeitgeist in himself . . . Everything about him had zest!

~Nancy Cunard, Hours Press

HOUDINI
by Bob Brown

Edited with an Introduction by
Craig Saper

ROVING EYE PRESS

Bad Ems — Cagnes-sur-mer — New York — Baltimore

Roving Eye Press

www.RovingEyePress.com

Roving Eye Press, initially founded in the late 1920s by Bob Brown and co-managed by his wife Rose, was part of a larger literary and artistic movement of small presses that served the modernist avant-garde. In 2014, a group of scholars and artists—with the support of Brown's descendents—relaunched the press and reissued its most important works. Its goal is to revitalize Bob Brown's reputation and importance for both twentieth century studies and our contemporary cultural scene.

Houdini was first published by Modern Editions Press, 1933.
A revised version appeared in *Prairie Schooner* 7.4 (Fall 1933).
Paperback edition ©2017 Roving Eye Press
Introduction ©2017 Craig Saper
Foreword ©2017 K. A. Wisniewski

ISBN 10: 0-692-99110-7
ISBN 13: 978-0-692-99110-7

Library of Congress Cataloging-in-Publication Data

Library of Congress Control Number: 2017962364

Book design and typesetting: O. U. Kidd & K. A. Wisniewski
Book cover: Kristina Markman

First paperback edition, December 2017

Printed in the United States of America.

CONTENTS

FOREWORD

It is impossible for me to read Bob Brown's work and not think of an often-overlooked part of literature and publishing: community. Few writers have contributed to so many different styles, modes, and artistic and literary movements and communities than Bob Brown. While scholars continue to be fascinated by his *readies* and the concept behind his reading machine, new researchers and artists alike are only now getting introduced to some of his other literary experiments. As readers will quickly recognize, perhaps his greatest experiment was not any single book or poem, but rather his lifelong pursuits in publishing.

Brown is the quintessential globe-glider—literally and metaphorically—constantly moving from one locale to the next and juggling numerous projects at a time. Although each place has its own set of challenges, he eagerly jumps into his new surroundings, quickly making friends with the most interesting of people and leaving his mark on the local scene before moving on. Similarly, his work demonstrates how Brown revels in the wonders and weirdness of the world around him. For Brown, publishing is a three-ring circus, or, perhaps more appropriately for this edition, a magic act. It is equal parts business, art, technology, education, performance, illusion, mediation, and meditation. Weaving through all of these dimensions, there are networks of friends, partners, colleagues, rivalries, editors, authors, artists, and readers. Brown understood, appreciated, and even helped construct such networks, most clearly visible in his work establishing the Associated Little Magazines, the Museum of Social Change, the Screen Writers Guild, and the Inter-American Museum Association.

To read Brown's works—whether its his collection of *Readies*, his censored *Gems*, his assemblage of recipes, or individual poems like "Houdini"—is to be served a piping hot medley of the most sweeping artistic and cultural ideas and experiences of his day. As a whole, these works showcase the massive transition underway both in publishing and twentieth-century culture. While some were widely circulated and wildly successful because of new technologies and promotional strategies implemented from the mass-market press, others celebrated the rise of the small press and little magazine and the freedom they offered to push aesthetics and design standards and distribute radical political and social criticisms.

"Houdini" was published in the middle of Brown's most productive period. From the late 1920s to the end of the 1930s, Brown published over thirty books and pamphlets. In the Introduction that follows, Craig Saper aptly notes, "Bob Brown was an escape artist." There is no easy way to define his work. During this period, he publishes novels and poetry, political manifestoes, cookbooks, and travel guides, and, more often than not, each work straddles the line between these genres. Some of these books were distributed by the largest commercial publishers of the period: Alfred A. Knopf; Farrar & Rinehart; Little, Brown, and Co.; Lippincott; and W. W. Norton. Others, like "Houdini" (Modern Editions, 1933), were published by small presses like Black Sun Press and Hours Press, which hosted some of the most innovative literary works of the day. And, finally, there's Roving Eye Press, Brown's own (mobile) press, which moved from Diessen to Bad Ems to Cagnes-sur-Mer in just over two years, and which produced his poetry collections *Globe-Gliding* (1930, published the following year as *Nomadness* by Dodd, Mead & Company), *The Readies* (1930) and *The Readies for Bob Brown's Machine* (1931), and *Gems: A Censored Anthology* (1931).

If there is a lesson to draw from this list, it is a willingness to play in and with all of these markets and networks and with both traditional and emerging forms, formats, and technologies. Saper, among others, has already illustrated the implications of individual works like *The Readies* on digital media and culture. As studies on the history of and best practices for current and future (digital) publishing expands, future scholars, too, will begin to more closely examine this period and Brown's contributions to it.

The origins of the word "publish," simply means to announce something or to make known. Over the past four years, I've tried to produce works that both reinvigorate Brown's works and ideals and recreate his experimental spirit. Just as Brown himself gifted many of the copies he produced, this second-coming of Roving Eye Press has mailed out hundreds of copies of titles for free to scholars, historians, artists, and institutions currently working in related fields. Furthermore, we've embraced the Open Access Movement and the latest trends in digital publishing by offering free PDF copies of all our titles for free at our website: http://www.RovingEyePress.com/. I am pleased that these works have been met with so much enthusiasm, and I think Brown would be pleased by our ongoing collaborations and group memberships, most recently with the Radical Open Access Collective.

If the world of small press publishing is magic, Bob Brown's poem "Houdini" is just another trick in our repertoire, another illusion to make sense of his world, and to make it whole. One Bob Brown sits backstage, raising his glass and shouting, "Huzzah!" Another is on stage, giving us all a wink. Another is at the . . . Now you see him; now you don't!

K. A. Wisniewski
Baltimore, MD

INTRODUCTION

Brown's *Houdini*: Allegory for Modern Times

By Craig Saper

In 1933, Bob Brown published his long poem, "Houdini," in The Modern Editions Press' Poetry Series[1] under the editorial direction of the under-appreciated Kathleen Tankersley Young (1903–1933), now known as a poet and editor closely associated with the Harlem Renaissance. Just before starting the pamphlet, Young also championed a blues-based poetry in her short-lived co-published magazine *Blues: A Magazine of New Rhymes* (1929-1930), with Charles Henry Ford and Parker Tyler. When Ford traveled to France in 1930, he met and befriended many in the expatriate avant-garde including Bob Brown. Brown included Ford's "Letter from the Provinces," and Young's "Love Story" in *Readies for Bob Brown's Machine* (1931). So, Brown's reputation as an impresario of literature by design, and the sense, among his peers including Young, that he was an "insane," wild, and "crazy gink," led Young to include him in the second poetry series.[2]

In the first of the two series, Young included "decorations" by modernist artists. Among these arists, Brown's good friend, Stuart Davis, included one of his prints in the first pamphlet. Davis and Brown were good friends since their time working together at *The Masses* in the 19-teens, and again in Paris among the avant-garde in the late 1920s. Kay Boyle, another one of Brown's closest friends among the expatriate avant-garde, wrote the poem for the third book in the series; the important modernist artist, Max Weber, contributed a print to the Boyle poem. Kathleen Tankersley Young was a key player for a few years among the American poetry scene and in regular communication with poets like William Carlos Williams, who was also a friend of Bob Brown's for many years. Later when Brown returned to the United States after fifteen years in exile, Young invited him to contribute to the series. "Houdini" would be among the last ever published by Young, as the series ended after her untimely death during a visit to Mexico. Young's own poem, "December Poet," has a line that gives a sense of the type of poetry she was looking for in her poetry series: "A new sound: although now vaguely familiar/And yet altogether strange".[3] Each series lasted one year. The second series comprised of Young's own poetry and a mix of expatriate avant-garde writers like Paul Bowles and Laurence Vail. It also included important cultural figures like Lincoln Kirstein who, with George Balanchine, had co-founded the New York City Ballet and the School of American Ballet; Horace Gregory, an important poet and translator; Raymond Ellsworth Larsson, a Midwestern modernist poet; and Carl Rakosi, known as what William Carlos Williams called an Objectivist poet, today not as well-known as Lorine Niedecker or Louis Zukofsky, who Young intended to include in a third series. Young included leading figures in American modernist poetry in both series included; they each sought that "new sound" that also illuminated the play of poetic structures in rhythms analogous to the modernist visual artists.

After 1931, the economic collapse had forced Brown to return to the United States, and, soon after he published *Houdini*, he would first join a radical labor commune, and then leave that group to teach at a labor college loosely associated with the commune. He continued to correspond with avant-garde writers, but his publications now included political tracts and cookbooks to keep food on the table. With Cora, his mother, and Rose, his wife, the Browns produced many bestselling cookbooks from the early 1930s through 1940s, and then again in the 1950s. When the Browns needed money, they made it anyway they could; when they had to flee, for political reasons in 1917, or wanted to explore the world as they did from 1926-1928, they moved to another city around the world: over a hundred cities outside of the United States. Bob Brown made and lost at least three fortunes in his lifetime, but he would always find some way to get by, usually by writing and selling books. Like many of his friends, he was constantly escaping from the cultural restraints. The U. S. government forced him and many of his friends into exile, as "slackers," for publishing anti-war statements in *The Masses*. Many among the expatriate avant-garde and a few of the contributors to Brown's *Readies* anthology, including Charles Henri Ford, were ostracized or fired from jobs at American universities for their bi- and homo-sexuality, which Ford and Parker Tyler celebrated in their important novel *The Young and Evil* (1933), the same year that Bob published his poem, and, of course, Kathleen Tankersley Young had to suffer the degradation and burden of being a black woman in America.

Bob founded a Museum of Social Change, in the mid-1930s, that sought to bring to consciousness the contradictions of wealth disparities that were literally killing the poor while the rich wallowed in excess and waste. Brown neither believed in, nor practiced, magic, and he railed against what we now call the secret powers of visualizing positive thinking. Houdini also bristled at the suggestion that he was a magician or that his escapes involved the supernatural. He was a skilled expert at his art. Neither Brown, nor Houdini, wanted to climb-up over others struggling to survive; they wanted to find a way out of the capitalist alienated labor practices through their expertise and artistic expression. Bob Brown was an escape artist.

Harry Houdini, the pseudonym of the famous escape artist, shared much in common with Brown. They both lived a version of the American dream that ran counter to rising-up the corporate or military ladder, but by escaping out of the tangle of chains and locked shackles of the workers and labor force including artists and writers. Bob Brown had helped start the Writers Guild to help writers protect and preserve their share of publication and performance rights; years earlier, in 1912, Brown had learned that the media owners and publishers had cheated him out of credit and profit for writing the first serialized movies ever made. Brown made it (and lost it) on his own terms. Like Houdini, Brown was making a fortune as a young man, which allowed him to travel, but once he discovered the freedom of the bohemians, radicals, and avant-garde artists, and, after meeting Marcel Duchamp after the Armory Exhibit and reading Gertrude Stein's *Tender Buttons*, he imagined throwing his typewriter into the air and exclaiming "Huzzah!" Likewise, Houdini was making a fortune by his early 30s. Once he had learned the showman's tricks, he was able to live life on his own terms rather than work his way up from laborer to manager to eventually become an owner.

Even though he had little money after he returned to the United States, Bob Brown was even more productive as a poet and essayist over the four years than he had been in the somewhat manic four years in Europe when he published multiple avant-garde poetry books, both with his own Roving Eye Press and with other presses like Nancy Cunard's Hours Press and Harry and Caresse Crosby's Black Sun Press, and inventing a wild reading machine. In the United States, he published short pieces in anthologies of Surrealist work in *Americans Abroad* in 1932, and, in 1933, he published essays and poems in *American Mercury*, *American Spectator*, *Americana*, *Panorama*, a Bob Brown issue of *Contempo*, *New Act: A Literary Review*, and even another earlier version of "Houdini" in *Prairie Schooner*.[4] He also published two booklets, including Houdini.

In the early 30s, the Browns got an advance from Little, Brown, and Company for a cookbook on using wine in recipes. Because they had already collected recipes during their stay in Europe, it was simply a matter of compiling the recipes and adding a smattering of discussion about national customs or combining foods. While in Atlantic Highlands, New Jersey, the Browns wrote that first, and most successful cookbook on *Cooking with Wine*, which in hindsight seems like a sure-fire commercial success, but at the time was a risky move as wine was something that winos drank on the street rather than as part of a sophisticated recipe for middle-class kitchens to keep in stock.

The work on "Houdini" consists of a series of scenes of how the magician created his own identity and the significance of his work: "shouldering loads of second hand rusty locks from the town dump lugging them home to practice on picking them as a maestro plucks strings making them a vibrant part of you," or working "alongside museum freaks" fraternizing with "the Dog-faced Boy" and "studying art in the gallery" and "on the Tattooed Lady's thighs." That Brown saw his own life among the avant-garde as something like a wonderful freak-show--not from the outside, but among--practicing his own art when he exclaims, "I but bend my finger in a beckon and birds, words of birds, hop on it, chirping," as Bob wrote as his subtitle to *Words* (Roving Eye Press, 1931).

These biographical details about Houdini also implicitly hint at Bob's own sense of his adventures as a magic act: "At the age of eight already a circus in yourself I see you always swinging in three three-rings ablaze from the parlor chandelier winking up peeks of strewn needles in the miraculous twitch of an eye." It is not by mere coincidence that Bob's autobiographical visual poem points to one eye with the caption, "My winking eye," and that he named his press "roving eye." Bob famously said, "words and I are one," but in this poem it is almost as if he is winking and saying, "Houdini and I are one," and that Houdini, the myth, is everyman up against the wall, tied up and under water, looking for an escape from a machine threatening to crush souls or drop us to the hard ground below--unless, with a pin hidden in your mouth, you pick the lock, twist impossibly out of a fix, and celebrate the possibility of your escape from the machinations of a strangulating situation some call work and the boss calls profit margins.

NOTES

[1] Bob Brown, *Houdini*, Poetry Series Pamphlet 8 (New York: The Modern Editions Press, 1933). The last in the publisher's Poetry Series, with 100-200 copies.

[2] Unpublished Letter from Kathleen Tankersley Young to Charles Henri Ford Papers, n.d., Charles Henri Ford Papers, Series II Correspondence: Kathleen Tankersley Young, TXRC97–A13, Box 16, Folder 6, the Harry Ransom Center, the University of Texas at Austin., "I was glad to hear - to get the book proffered by the insane Bob Brown - to hear to get anything to prove the reality of existence beyond this pool of blackness." Kathleen Tankersley Young to Charles Henri Ford Papers, n.d., Charles Henri Ford Papers, Series II Correspondence: Kathleen Tankersley Young, TXRC97–A13, Box 16, Folder 6, the Harry Ransom Center, the University of Texas at Austin. Unpublished Letter to Kathleen Tankersley Young about Bob Brown from Ruth Widen (March 25, 1931), 2. "We got an order from that crazy gink in Paris, whatsisname, Bob Brown? and the bank tells us we can have $1.95 for his francs––not so bad, only 30¢ off for cashing a French check."

[3] Kathleen Tankersly Young, "December Portrait," *Opportunity* (December 1930): 360.

[4] In chronological order, Brown published the following works after returning to the United States: "Pages from the Book of Beer," *American Mercury*, 26 (June 1932): 185-191. "Drug-store in a Dry Town," *American Mercury*, 26 (August 1932): 405-41; *Contempo: A Review of Books and Personalities*, special Brown issue, includes essays and poems by Brown, 2 (31 August 1932); "Report of a Returned New Yorker," *American Mercury*, 27 (October 1932): 185-192; "Swell Days for Literary Guys," *American Mercury*, 27 (December 1932): 480-485; "Houdini," *Prairie Schooner*, 7 (Fall 1933): 156-158; "Them Asses," *American Mercury*, 30 (December

1933): 403-411; "Greenwich Village Gallops," *American Mercury*, 31 (January 1934): 103-111; "Kelly" (a story), *The New Act: A Literary Review*, No. 3 (April 1934), ed. H. R. Hays and Harold Rosenberg.

HOUDINI

BOB BROWN

Roving Eye Press

Bad Ems — Cagnes-sur-Mer — New York — Baltimore

HOUDINI

Houdini; you are the loaves and the fishes
self-contained three-ring circus
hanging from the chandelier
by your rosined pink heels
you pick up needles from the parlor carpet
with lightning lashes
in the thunderous clap of an eye

at the miraculous age of eight
scattering breathless wonders upside down

materializing your stage name
out of a second-hand copy of
The Works of Robert Houdin
French diplomat and master magician
inhaling the exact name for you
snatching it full-blown out of thin air
with a deep-sweeping bow

Houdini; I see you shouldering loads of
second hand rusty locks
from the town dump
lugging them home to practice on
picking them as a maestro plucks strings
making them a vibrant part of you

Houdini; I see you shouldering loads of
second hand rusty locks
from the town dump
lugging them home to practice on
picking them as a maestro plucks strings
making them a vibrant part of you

As a youth doing your turn
alongside museum freaks
fraternizing with the Dog-faced Boy
studying art in the gallery
on the Tattooed Lady's thighs
feeding nails to the Human Ostrich
hollaring This Way, Ladies and Gents
All For a Thin Dime!

You, American Indian medicine man and
Salem witch spiritualist by turns

Wrapping the Bearded Lady's sneezing pug
in a warm side-show blanket
tucking it all cuddle-cozy into
The Marvellous Midget's thumb-nail bed
untying knots with your toes for practice
ripping endless needles out of your mouth
whetting the Sword-Swallower's knives
keeping the hand sharper than the eye
heating nursing bottles for
The Hoboken Siamese Twins
making finger-noses at Grimm
The Fairytale Giant.

Hush, Houdini: you are as much an American miracle
as Edgar Allan Poe
as great a prodigy and pride
acclaimed in Paris, Berlin, and Budapest
mystifier of misty jail wardens
now they see you, now they don't!

Caught in a spider web of chains
an upside-down ceiling fly
padlocked grinding chin to knocking knees
locked naked as a Follies girl
into the warden's surest cell
in eight minutes by the town clock
you appear all bows and smiles
fully dressed as an archbishop
on the stage of your awed theatre
a mile and a half away

Blindfold watch-number reader
every trick in the pack for you,
picker of pockets and padlocks
finder of needles in hay-stacks

At the age of eight
already a circus in yourself
I see you always swinging in three rings
ablaze from the parlor chandelier
winking up pecks of strewn needles
in the miraculous twitch of an eye.

ABOUT THE AUTHOR

Robert Carlton "Bob" Brown (1886-1959) was an American writer and publisher in many forms. In the first two decades of the twentieth century, Brown was a bestselling fiction writer, selling hundreds of stories to magazines and collecting some of these for the collections *What Happened to Mary?* (1913) and *The Remarkable Adventures of Christopher Poe* (1913). By the end of the decade, he became a central figure of the Bohemian arts scene in Greenwich Village and published two books of poetry *Tahiti: 10 Rhythms* (1915) and *My Majonary* (1916). After nearly a decade of traveling the globe, in 1928 Brown and his wife Rose joined the expatriate avant-garde in France, where he conducted his most famous and experimental works. These included *1450-1950* (1929), *The Readies* (1930), *Words* (1931), and *Gems: A Censored Anthology* (1931). In the 1930s, the Browns entered a new phase in their writing careers as bestselling cookbook authors and moved to Hollywood to write story treatments. Bob Brown spent the last years of his life in New York City, devoted to collecting rare books and publishing and collaborating with writers from the emerging Beat movement.

ABOUT THE EDITOR

Craig Saper is the author of *The Amazing Adventures of Bob Brown* (2016), *Intimate Bureaucracies* (2012), *Networked Art* (2001), and *Artificial Mythologies* (1997) and editor or co-editor of *Electracy: Gregory L. Ulmer's Textshop Experiments* (2015), *Hyperrhiz's* "Mapping Culture Multimodally" (2015), and special issues of *Rhizomes* on "Posthumography" (2010), "Imaging Place" (2009), and "Drifts" (2007). He also edited and introduced new editions of Bob Brown's *Readies* (2014), *Words* (2014), *Gems* (2014), and *1450-1950* (2015). Saper's curatorial projects include exhibits on *Noigandres: Concrete Poetry in Brazil* (1988), *Assemblings* (1997), *Folkvine.org* (2003-2006), and *Typebound* (2008). He is Professor of Language, Literacy & Culture at UMBC and co-founder of Electric Press.

Other titles by Roving Eye Press

The Readies
Words
Gems: A Censored Anthology
1450-1950

Other titles by Bob Brown

The Remarkable Adventures of Christopher Poe
What Happened to Mary
Tahiti : 10 Rhythms
My Marjonary
Globe-Gliding
Nomadness
Readies for Bob Brown's Machine
Let There Be Beer!
Homemade Hilarity
Can We Co-Operate?
The Complete Book of Cheese
14 Poets, 1 Artist

(with Rose Brown)

Amazing Amazon

(with Rose & Cora Brown)
The European Cookbook for American Homes
10,000 Snacks
The Country Cookbook
Salads and Herbs
Soups, Sauces, and Gravies
The Vegetable Cook Book
Most for Your Money Cookbook
Outdoor Cooking
The South American Cook Book

Roving Eye Press

www.ingramcontent.com/pod-product-compliance
Lightning Source LLC
Chambersburg PA
CBHW060552030426
42337CB00019B/3527